I0823436

For Tim,
my forever soulmate and eternal love.

Sanny Winters

LOVE LETTERS

Lannoo

AT FIRST SIGHT

The Unbearable Lightness of Being

Milan Kundera

1984

I have been thinking about Tomas for many years, but not until I saw him in the light of a new perception did I see him clearly. I saw him standing at the window of his flat and looking across the courtyard at the opposite walls, not knowing what to do.

He had first met Tereza about three weeks earlier in a small Czech town. They had spent scarcely an hour together. She had accompanied him to the station and waited with him until he boarded the train. Ten days later she paid him a visit. They made love the day she arrived. That night she came down with a fever, and stayed a whole week in his flat with the flu.

He had come to feel an inexplicable love for this all but complete stranger; she seemed a child to him, a child someone had laid in a bulrush basket daubed with pitch, and sent downstream for Tomas to fetch at the riverbank of his bed.

Eleanor Oliphant is Completely Fine

Gail Honeyman

2017

I have always taken great pride in managing my life alone. I'm a sole survivor - I'm Eleanor Oliphant. I don't need anyone else - there's no big hole in my life, no missing part of my own particular puzzle. I am a self-contained entity. That's what I've always told myself, at any rate. But last night, I'd found the love of my life. When I saw him walk on stage, I just knew.

LOVEBIRDS

Narcissus and Goldmund

Hermann Hesse

1930

Quietly he let the streams flow through him; happily he felt the boundless fire grow, felt it alive in both of them, turning their little lair into the vital, breathing center of all the quiet night.

He bent over Lise's face and began to kiss her lips in the darkness. Suddenly he saw her eyes and forehead shine with a gentle light. He looked in surprise, watched the glow grow brighter, more intense. Then he knew and turned his head: the moon was rising over the edge of the long black stretch of forest. He watched the white gentle light miraculously inundate her forehead, her cheeks, slide over her round, limpid throat. Softly, delighted, he said: 'How beautiful you are!'

A Man from Her Past

Lydia Davis

2007

I think Mother is flirting with a man from her past who is not Father. I say to myself: Mother ought not to have improper relations with this man "Franz"! "Franz" is a European. I say she should not see this man improperly while Father is away! But I am confusing an old reality with a new reality: Father will not be returning home. He will be staying on at Vernon Hall. As for Mother, she is ninety-four years old. How can there be improper relations with a woman of ninety-four? Yet my confusion must be this: though her body is old, her capacity for betrayal is still young and fresh.

CUPID

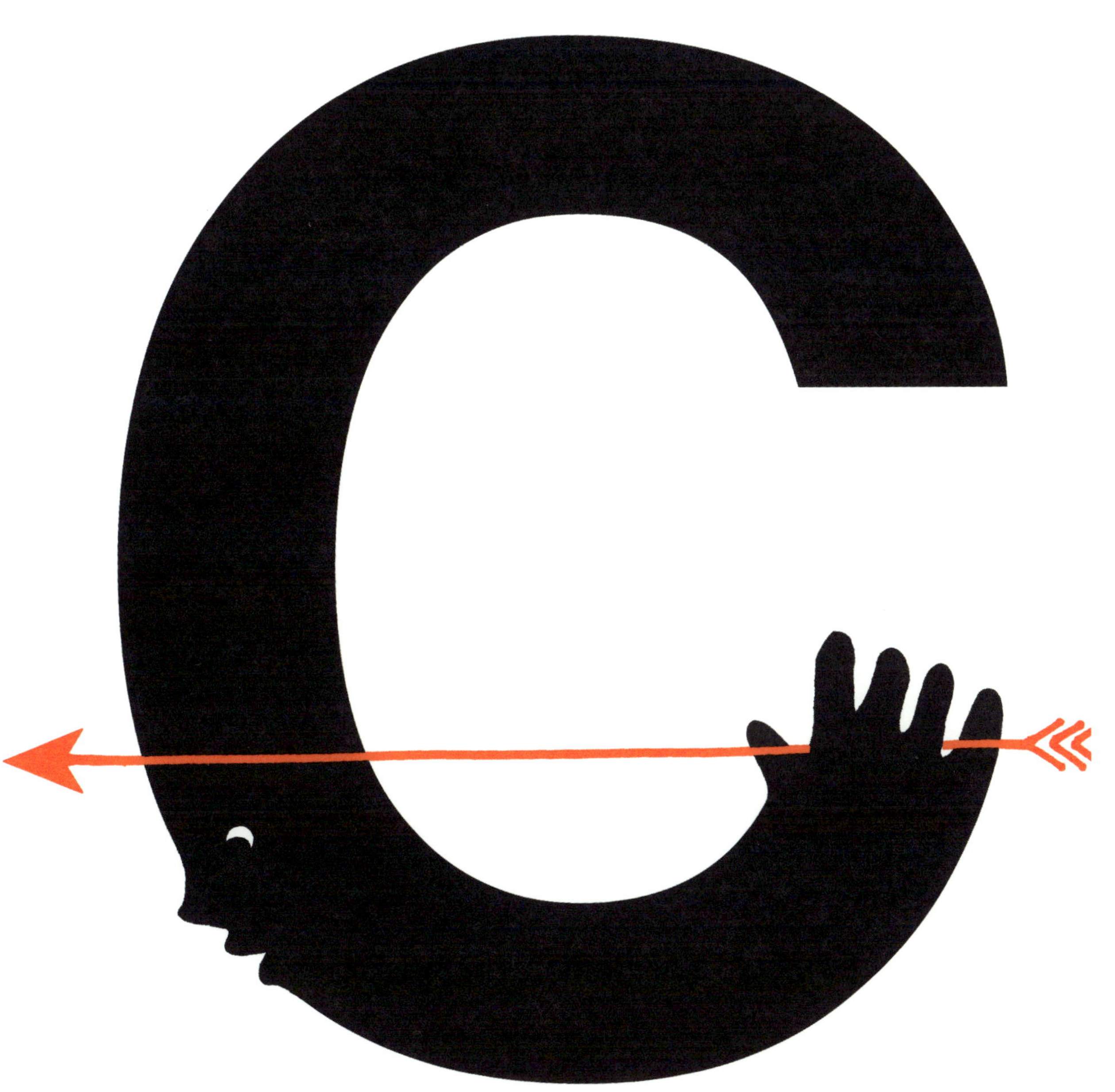

Mrs Dalloway

Virginia Woolf

1925

"In love," he repeated, now speaking rather dryly to Clarissa Dalloway; "in love with a girl in India." He had deposited his garland. Clarissa could make what she would of it.
"In love!" she said. That he at his age should be sucked under in his little bow-tie by that monster! And there's no flesh on his neck; his hands are red; and he's six months older than I am! her eye flashed back to her; but in her heart she felt, all the same, he is in love. He has that, she felt; he is in love.
But the indomitable egotism which for ever rides down the hosts opposed to it, the river which says on, on, on; even though, it admits, there may be no goal for us whatever, still on, on; this indomitable egotism charged her cheeks with colour; made her look very young; very pink; very bright-eyed as she sat with her dress upon her knee, and her needle held to the end of green silk, trembling a little. He was in love! Not with her. With some younger woman, of course.
"And who is she?" she asked.
Now this statue must be brought from its height and set down between them.
"A married woman, unfortunately," he said; "the wife of a Major in the Indian Army."
And with a curious ironical sweetness he smiled as he placed her in this ridiculous way before Clarissa.
(All the same, he is in love, thought Clarissa.)

Fireworks

Jan Lauwereyns

2002

According to the astronomer standing there
with a mouthful of teeth – smart fellow –
there was something already in the beginning.

Something: with great gravitational force,
a black hole, a flame in my heart.

If not, no event t before t + 1,
and so nothing between the two

where time could

take place. And without time
no arrow that leaves somewhere in order to
God knows when arrive somewhere else.

God, Cupid, Thor.

So we silently think
there must have begun something
that was the beginning of it all.

DATE

The Hour of the Star
Clarice Lispector

1977

They didn't know how to take a walk. They walked through the heavy rain and stopped in front of a hardware store where the window display featured piping, tin cans, large bolts and nails. And Macabéa, afraid that the silence might already mean separation, said to her new boyfriend:

--I just love bolts and nails, what about you, sir?

The second time they met a soft drizzle was falling that soaked them to the bone. Without even holding hands they walked in the rain that on Macabéa's face looked like flowing tears.

The third time they met – wouldn't you know it was raining? – the guy, irritated and losing the light varnish of politeness that his stepfather had taught him with great effort, said:

--All you ever do is rain!

--I'm sorry!

But she already loved him so much that she could no longer do without him, she was desperately in love.

Once when they met she finally asked his name.

--Olímpico de Jesus Moreira Chaves – he lied because his only last name was de Jesus, name of those who have no father. He'd been raised by a stepfather who taught him smooth ways of dealing with people in order to take advantage of them and how to pick up girls.

--I don't understand your name – she said. – Olímpico?

Macabéa feigned enormous curiosity hiding from him that

she never understood anything very well and that was just how it was. But he little fighting cock that he was, bristled at the stupid question to which he didn't know the answer. He said annoyed:

--I know but I don't want to tell you!

--It doesn't matter, it doesn't matter, it doesn't matter ... we don't need to know what our names mean.

ETERNAL LOVE

Romeo and Juliet

Shakespeare

1597

For never was a story of more woe, Than this of Juliet and her Romeo.

Levels of Life

Julian Barnes

2013

You put together two people who have not been put together before. Sometimes it is like that first attempt to harness a hydrogen balloon to a fire balloon: do you prefer crash and burn, or burn and crash? But sometimes it works, and something new is made, and the world is changed. Then, at some point, sooner or later, for this reason or that, one of them is taken away. And what is taken away is greater than the sum of what was there. This may not be mathematically possible; but it is emotionally possible.

Funeral Blues

W.H. Auden

1940

Stop all the clocks, cut off the telephone.
Prevent the dog from barking with a juicy bone,
Silence the pianos and with muffled drum
Bring out the coffin, let the mourners come.

Let aeroplanes circle moaning overhead
Scribbling in the sky the message He is Dead,
Put crêpe bows round the white necks of the public doves,
Let the traffic policemen wear black cotton gloves.

He was my North, my South, my East and West,
My working week and my Sunday rest
My noon, my midnight, my talk, my song;
I thought that love would last forever, I was wrong.

The stars are not wanted now; put out every one,
Pack up the moon and dismantle the sun.
Pour away the ocean and sweep up the wood;
For nothing now can ever come to any good.

FIRST LOVE

Americanah

Chimamanda Ngozi Adichie

2013

During her first year in America, when she took New Jersey Transit to Penn Station and then the subway to visit Aunty Uju in Flatlands, she was struck by how mostly slim white people got off at the stops in Manhattan and, as the train went further into Brooklyn, the people left were mostly black and fat. She had not thought of them as "fat," though. She had thought of them as "big," because one of the first things her friend Ginika told her was that "fat" in America was a bad word, heaving with moral judgment like "stupid" or "bastard," and not a mere description like "short" or "tall." So she had banished "fat" from her vocabulary. But "fat" came back to her last winter, after almost thirteen years, when a man in line behind her at the supermarket muttered, "Fat people don't need to be eating that shit," as she paid for her giant bag of Tostitos. She glanced at him, surprised, mildly offended, and thought it a perfect blog post, how this stranger had decided she was fat. She would file the post under the tag "race, gender and body size." But back home, as she stood and faced the mirror's truth, she realized that she had ignored, for too long, the new tightness of her clothes, the rubbing together of her inner thighs, the softer, rounder parts of her that shook when she moved. She was fat.

She said the word "fat" slowly, funneling it back and forward, and thought about all the other things she had learned not to say aloud in America. She was fat. She was not curvy or big-boned; she was fat, it was the only word that felt true. And she had ignored, too, the cement in her soul. Her blog was doing well, with thousands of unique visitors each month, and she was earning good speaking fees, and she had a fellowship at Princeton and a relationship with Blaine—"You are the absolute love of my life," he'd written in her last birthday card—and yet there was cement in her soul. It had been there for a while, an early morning disease of fatigue, a bleakness and borderlessness. It brought with it amorphous longings, shapeless desires, brief imaginary glints of other lives she could be living, that over the months melded into a piercing homesickness. She scoured Nigerian websites, Nigerian profiles on Facebook, Nigerian blogs, and each click brought yet another story of a young person who had recently moved back home, clothed in American or British degrees, to start an investment company, a music production business, a fashion label, a magazine, a fast-food franchise. She looked at photographs of these men and women and felt the dull ache of loss, as though they had prised open her hand and taken something of hers. They were living her life. Nigeria became where she was supposed to be, the only place she could sink her roots in without the constant urge to tug them out and shake off the soil. And, of course, there was also Obinze. Her first love, her first lover, the only person with whom she had never felt the need to explain herself.

GAY LOVE

Giovanni's Room

James Baldwin

1956

But this time when I touched him something happened in him and in me which made this touch different from any touch either of us had ever known. And he did not resist, as he usually did, but lay where I had pulled him, against my chest. And I realized that my heart was beating in an awful way and that Joey was trembling against me and the light in the room was very bright and hot. I started to move and to make some kind of joke but Joey mumbled something and I put my head down to hear. Joey raised his head as I lowered mine and we kissed, as it were, by accident. Then, for the first time in my life, I was really aware of another person's body, of another person's smell. We had our arms around each other. It was like holding in my hand some rare, exhausted, nearly doomed bird which I had miraculously happened to find. I was very frightened; I am sure he was frightened too, and we shut our eyes. To remember it so clearly, so painfully tonight tells me that I have never for an instant truly forgotten it. I feel in myself now a faint, a dreadful stirring of what so overwhelmingly stirred in me then, great thirsty heat, and trembling, and tenderness so painful I thought my heart would burst. But out of this astounding, intolerable pain came joy; we gave each other joy that night. It seemed, then, that a lifetime would not be long enough for me to act with Joey the act of love.

Lie With Me

Philippe Besson

2017

Love, it's mouths that seek, lips that bite, drawing a little blood. His stubble irritates my chin, his hands grab my jaw so that I can't escape.

It's the coarseness of his hair where I slide my fingers, the tautness of his neck. My arms close around him, encircle him to be as close as possible, so that there is no space between us.

It's torsos that join together and then withdraw in a hurry to remove clothing, the Nordic sweater, the T-shirt, so that finally it's skin next to skin. His torso is muscular and hairless, with nipples that are flat and dark. My chest is skinny, not yet deformed as it will be four years later by the blows of an emergency room doctor.

It's skin that is frantically caressed. My fingers find a constellation of moles, just as I guessed, on his back.

It's jeans that we unbutton. I discover his sex, veiny, white, sumptuous. I am enthralled by his sex. It will take many years and many lovers before I ever return to this sense of amazement.

Love, it's taking each other in the mouth, maintaining a certain comportment despite the frenzy. It's exercising restraint not to come, the excitement is so powerful. It's abandonment, that crazy trust in the other.

HORNY

The Story of My Teeth

Valeria Luiselli

2013

Allegoric lot n°3
Rat and mouse costumes

The young lady Valeria Luiselli, a mediocre high school student, stammered and overused the suffix –ly. As her parents, Mrs. Weiss and Mr. Fischli, wanted her to give a speech at her fifteenth birthday party, they sent her to singing, elocution, and public speaking classes. Her party was to be a very elegant celebration in the neighborhood dance hall, and the girl needed to prepare herself for the occasion.

For the elocution and public speaking classes, they hired the famous teacher Guillermo Sheridan. The first sentence that Professor Guillermo Sheridan taught Valeria Luiselli to say was: "Titus Livy had a conk like a coconut and Octavio Paz was a big head." Despite the shortness and simplicity of the sentence, it took the young girl a lot of effort to pronounce it correctly. Every time she made a mistake, Professor Guillermo Sheridan would hit her on the palm of the hand with a cane. The girl had to repeat the same sentence 112 times before her teacher called an end to the first session.

That night, while they were eating a dinner of octopus a la gallega with white rice, the girl's parents asked her how her first public speaking class had gone, and if she had learned anything useful that she would like to share with them. The young girl said:

Titus Livy was a cokehead.

What's that, my girl? asked her father.

Titus Livy was a cokehead, repeated the adolescent.

Valeria Luiselli's parents looked each other in the eyes and ate the rest of their octopus in silence.

That night, the young girl's progenitors put on their plush rat and mouse costumes, and, instead of reading or watching television, as they did almost every other night, they committed an act of outlandish, noisy, uninterrupted coitus. When they had finished, still half-dressed in their costumes, the couple lay silently staring at the ceiling.

ILLUSION

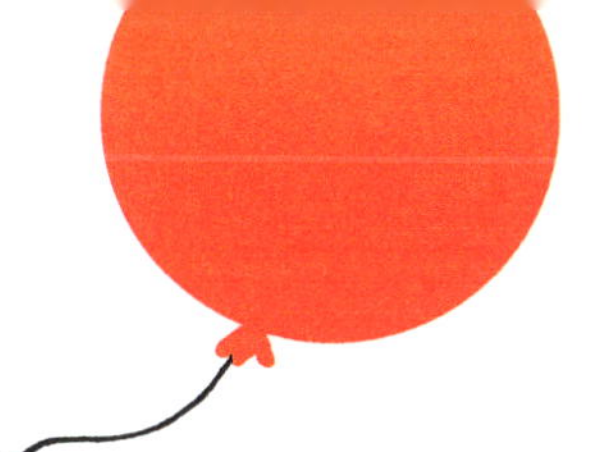

The Infatuations

Javier Marías

2012

'That's the mistake people make,' he said after a few seconds, without looking away or changing his posture, as though, rather than speaking, he was waiting, 'a childish mistake that many adults cling to until the day they die, as if throughout their entire existence they had failed to grasp how things work, as if they lacked all experience. The mistake of believing that the present is for ever, that what happens in each moment is definitive, when we should all know that as long as we still have a little time left, nothing is definitive. We have all experienced enough twists and turns, not just in terms of luck but as regards our state of mind. We gradually learn that what seems really important now will one day seem a mere fact, a neutral piece of information. We learn that there will come a time when we don't even give a thought to the person we once couldn't live without and over whom we spent sleepless nights, without whom life seemed impossible, on whose words and presence we depended day after day, and if we ever do, very occasionally, give that person a thought, it will merely be to shrug and think at most: "I wonder what became of her?" without a flicker of concern or curiosity.

The Sorrows of Young Werther

Johann Wolfgang Goethe

1774

Charlotte had slept little during the past night. All her apprehensions were realised in a way that she could neither foresee nor avoid. Her blood was boiling in her veins, and a thousand painful sensations rent her pure heart. Was it the ardour of Werther's passionate embraces that she felt within her bosom? Was it anger at his daring? Was it the sad comparison of her present condition with former days of innocence, tranquillity, and self-confidence? How could she approach her husband, and confess a scene which she had no reason to conceal, and which she yet felt, nevertheless, unwilling to avow? They had preserved so long a silence toward each other and should she be the first to break it by so unexpected a discovery? She feared that the mere statement of Werther's visit would trouble him, and his distress would be heightened by her perfect candour. She wished that he could see her in her true light, and judge her without prejudice; but was she anxious that he should read her inmost soul? On the other hand, could she deceive a being to whom all her thoughts had ever been exposed as clearly as crystal, and from whom no sentiment had ever been concealed? These reflections made her anxious and thoughtful. Her mind still dwelt on Werther, who was now lost to her, but whom she could not bring herself to resign, and for whom she knew nothing was left but despair if she should be lost to him for ever.

JEALOUS

The Story of a New Name

Elena Ferrante

2012

Antonio's fixation was always the same: Sarratore's son {Nino}. He was afraid that I would talk to him, even that I would see him {at school}. Naturally, to prevent him from suffering, I concealed the fact that I ran into Nino entering school, coming out, in the corridors. Nothing particularly happened, at most we exchanged a nod of greeting and went on our way: I could have talked to my boyfriend about it without any problems if he had been a reasonable person. But Antonio was not reasonable and in truth I wasn't either.

The Dangers of Smoking in Bed

Mariana Enriquez

2009

That weekend when we went to the quarry pool they were holding hands, and we just couldn't understand it. We couldn't understand it. The red bikini with hearts on one of us; the super-flat stomach with a belly button piercing on another; the exquisite haircut that fell just so over the face, legs without a single hair, underarms like marble. And he preferred her? Why? Because he screwed her? But we wanted to screw too, that was all we wanted!

KISS

Conversations with Friends

Sally Rooney

2017

Remember the first time we kissed? he said. At the party. And I said I didn't think the utility room was a good place to be kissing and we left. You know I went up to my room and waited for you, right? I mean for hours. And at first I really thought you would come. It was probably the most wretched I ever felt in my life, this kind of ecstatic wretchedness that in a way I was practically enjoying. Because even if you did come upstairs, what then? The house was full of people, it's not like anything was going to happen. But every time I thought of going back down again I would imagine hearing you on the stairs, and I couldn't leave, I mean I physically couldn't. Anyway, how I felt then, knowing that you were close by and feeling completely paralyzed by it, this phone call was similar. If I told you where my car was right now, I don't think I'd be able to leave, I think I would have to stay here just in case you changed your mind about everything. You know, I still have that impulse to be available to you. You'll notice I didn't buy anything in the supermarket.

I closed my eyes. Things and people moved around me, taking positions in obscure hierarchies, participating in systems I didn't know about and never would. A complex network of objects and concepts. You live through certain things before you understand them. You can't always take the analytic position.

Come and get me, I said.

Swann's Way

Marcel Proust

1913

He would make Odette play him the phrase again, ten, twenty times on end, insisting that, while she played, she must never cease to kiss him. Every kiss provokes another. Ah, in those earliest days of love how naturally the kisses spring into life.

LESBIAN LOVE

Fragment 105

Sappho

c. 500 BC

Fragment 105(a)

You: an Achilles' apple
Blushing sweet on a high branch
At the tip of the tallest tree.
You escaped those who would
pluck your fruit.
Not that they didn't try. No,
They could not forget you
Poised beyond their reach.

Fragment 105(c)

O my mountain hyacinth
What shepherds trod upon you
With clumsy, rustic foot?
Now you are a broken seal:
A scarlet stain upon the earth.

MISS YOU

If You Were Coming in the Fall

Emily Dickinson

1890

VI.
If you were coming in the fall,
I'd brush the summer by
With half a smile and half a spurn,
As housewives do a fly.

If I could see you in a year,
I'd wind the months in balls,
And put them each in separate drawers,
Until their time befalls.

If only centuries delayed,
I'd count them on my hand,
Subtracting till my fingers dropped
Into Van Diemen's land.

If certain, when this life was out,
That yours and mine should be,
I'd toss it yonder like a rind,
And taste eternity.

But now, all ignorant of the length
Of time's uncertain wing,
It goads me, like the goblin bee,
That will not state its sting.

Open Water

Caleb Azumah Nelson

2021

You are ending summer, hands resting on each other's thighs. Sitting across from each other on the train home, you were holding a gaze you could be forgiven for suggesting will never break. In moments such as these, time acts as it does in your relationship, falling away; past, present and future melding in the warmth of our touch. Neither of you wish to let this gaze go, but you know you must, if only briefly, knowing the return is an inevitability.

Later, lying in bed together, the feeling of timelessness heavier now you have come to a halt. This moment seems to be going on forever. What is it Kierkegaard says of the difference between a moment and an instant, of the fullness of time? Unimportant, as you fumble in the dark, knowing each other fully, in a way which will not be forgotten, in a way which feels right.

You are ending the summer, wondering how it is possible to miss someone before they have gone. There are lives moving around you but they are of little concern. Leaning against a noticeboard, your arms around her, running your chin over the softness of her shorn blonde head. You're both watching nervously for her train platform to be announced, and right on time –

'That's you', you say.

'That's me,' she says.

NARCISSISM

American Psycho

Bret Easton Ellis

1991

Before leaving my office for the meeting I take two Valium, wash them down with a Perrier and then use a scruffing cleanser on my face with premoistened cotton balls, afterwards applying a moisturizer. I'm wearing a wool tweed suit and a striped cotton shirt, both by Yves Saint Laurent, and a silk tie by Armani and new black cap-toed shoes by Ferragamo. I Plax then brush my teeth and when I blow my nose, thick, ropy strings of blood and snot stain a forty-five-dollar handkerchief from Hermès that, unfortunately, wasn't a gift. But I've been drinking close to twenty liters of Evian water a day and going to the tanning salon regularly and one night of binging hasn't affected my skin's smoothness or color tone. My complexion is still excellent. Three drops of Visine clear the eyes. An ice pack tightens the skin. All it comes down to is: I feel like shit but look great.

Mythos

Stephen Fry

2017

Hot and thirsty from all the stress and drama he knelt down to drink from the stream. He caught his breath in astonishment when in its waters, he saw the loveliest face he had ever laid eyes upon, the sweet and surprised face of a most beautiful young man. He had golden hair and soft red lips. Narcissus recognized with a thrill that the youth's beguiling and loving eyes had the hungry, needy look he had always found so repellent in others. But the very same expression on the gorgeous face of this mysterious stranger made Narcissus's chest swell and heart thump with joy. It must mean that the glorious creature in the river felt the same way as he did! Narcissus leaned down to kiss the lovely lips and the lovely lips came up to kiss his, but just as Narcissus lowered his face, the stranger's features broke into a thousand dancing, rippling pieces until he could see them no longer and Narcissus found he was kissing nothing but cold water.

"Stay still, lovely one," he breathed, and the boy seemed to whisper the same to him.

OPPOSITES ATTRACT

Girl, Woman, Other

Bernardine Evaristo

2019

who was this woman letting her son-in-law do her every which way?

who was this woman who took him into her mouth and enjoyed it? when the only time she did it to Clovis she had thrown up afterwards?

who was this woman who kept up with this young man who exploded multiple times inside her because he was virile and could go on forever and so could she until they died from exhaustion because she was completely out of her mind and inside her body?

until
the alarm in the kitchen went
she had to collect Karen and Rachel from the nursery
they showered and dressed themselves
left the house
separately
him
first

that night she couldn't sleep
she went to war with her morals on behalf of her feelings
guess which side won?
she was nearly fifty
she deserved to have this
him

The Prophet

Kahlil Gibran

1923

Love one another, but make not a bond of love.
Let it rather be a moving sea between the shores of your souls.
Fill each other's cup, but drink not from one cup.
Give one another of your bread, but eat not from the same loaf.
Sing and dance together and be joyous, but let each one of you
be alone.
Even as the strings of a lute are alone though they quiver with
the same music.
Give your hearts, but not into each other's keeping.
For only the hand of life can contain your hearts.
And stand together, yet not too near together.

POLYAMORY

Another Roadside Attraction

Tom Robbins

1971

As long as it's done with honesty and grace, John Paul doesn't mind if I go to bed with other men. Or with other girls, as is sometimes my fancy. What has marriage got to do with it? Marriage is not a synonym for monogamy any more than monogamy is a synonym for ideal love. To live lightly on the earth, lovers and families must be more flexible and relaxed. The ritual of sex releases its magic inside or outside the marital bond. I approach that ritual with as much humility as possible and perform it whenever it seems appropriate. As for John Paul and me, a strange spurt of semen is not going to wash our love away.

The Myth of Sisyphus

Albert Camus

1942

Whence each woman hopes to give him what no one has ever given him. Each time they are utterly wrong and merely manage to make him feel the need of that repetition. “At last,” exclaims one of them, “I have given you love.” Can we be surprised that Don Juan laughs at this? “At last? No,” he says, “but once more.” Why should it be essential to love rarely in order to love much?

QUEEN OF HEARTS

Little Snow-White

Jacob and Wilhelm Grimm

1812

Not long afterward she opened her eyes, lifted the lid from her coffin, sat up, and was alive again.

"Good heavens, where am I?" she cried out.

The prince said joyfully, "You are with me." He told her what had happened, and then said, "I love you more than anything else in the world. Come with me to my father's castle. You shall become my wife." Snow-White loved him, and she went with him. Their wedding was planned with great splendor and majesty.

Snow-White's godless stepmother was also invited to the feast. After putting on her beautiful clothes she stepped before her mirror and said:

Mirror, mirror, on the wall,
Who in this land is fairest of all?

The mirror answered:

You, my queen, are fair; it is true.
But the young queen is a thousand times fairer than you.

Black Hole Sun

Peter Verhelst

2008

2.
We were not useful, jewels, and squandered luxuries,
Our love consumed itself as it burned,
We gave and took with sheer abandon, boundaries
Unknown to us, the thing we never learned

Was not to tell, why should we, lovers rather handle
What's abundant, being boys who managed to conjure
Gold from flesh and muscle. Flickering flames on a candle
Burning at both ends. Something halfway a creature

And God. Both greedy and needy. Crazy. Two kingly serpents
In a mating dance that seemed eternal; nothing
Is eternal though, my love: eternity is desire's burden,

Of which we were aware, we wanted that in all respects,
To be exhausted by us rather than washed out. It's all or nothing.
You are my all. Take me. From smile to sex.

RED

The Spanish Dancer

Rainer Maria Rilke

1918

As a lit match first flickers in the hands
Before it flames, and darts out from all sides
Bright, twitching tongues, so, ringed by growing bands
Of spectators—she, quivering, glowing stands
Poised tensely for the dance—then forward glides

And suddenly becomes a flaming torch.
Her bright hair flames, her burning glances scorch,
And with a daring art at her command
Her whole robe blazes like a fire-brand
From which is stretched each naked arm, awake,
Gleaming and rattling like a frightened snake.

And then, as though the fire fainter grows,
She gathers up the flame—again it glows,
As with proud gesture and imperious air
She flings it to the earth; and it lies there
Furiously flickering and crackling still—
Then haughtily victorious, but with sweet
Swift smile of greeting, she puts forth her will
And stamps the flames out with her small firm feet.

Salomé

Oscar Wilde

1893

It is thy mouth that I desire, Jokanaan. Thy mouth is like a band of scarlet on a tower of ivory. It is like a pomegranate cut with a knife of ivory. The pomegranate-flowers that blossom in the gardens of Tyre, and are redder than roses, are not so red. The red blasts of trumpets that herald the approach of kings, and make afraid the enemy, are not so red. Thy mouth is redder than the feet of those who tread the wine in the wine-press. Thy mouth is redder than the feet of the doves who haunt the temples and are fed by the priests. It is redder than the feet of him who cometh from a forest where he hath slain a lion, and seen gilded tigers. Thy mouth is like a branch of coral that fishers have found in the twilight of the sea, the coral that they keep for the kings!... It is like the vermilion that the Moabites find in the mines of Moab, the vermilion that the kings take from them. It is like the bow of the King of the Persians, that is painted with vermilion, and is tipped with coral. There is nothing in the world so red as thy mouth....

Let me kiss thy mouth.

SOULMATES

Embers

Sándor Márai

1942

"Do you also believe that what gives our lives their meaning is the passion that suddenly invades us heart, soul, and body, and burns in us forever, no matter what else happens in our lives? And that if we have experienced this much, then perhaps we haven't lived in vain? Is passion so deep and terrible and magnificent and inhuman? Is it indeed about desiring any one person, or is it about desiring desire itself? That is the question. Or perhaps, is it indeed about desiring a particular person, a single, mysterious other, once and for always, no matter whether that person is good or bad, and the intensity of our feelings bears no relation to that individual's qualities or behavior?"

The Symposium

Plato

c. 385 - 370 B.C. (?)

And when one of them meets the other half of his own soul, the pair are lost in an amazement of love and friendship and intimacy. And if the man is the right one, the woman will be his soulmate; if the woman is the right one, the man will be hers. For they were originally one, and the division into two halves was done by the gods to create a perfect union. Now, when the two halves are reunited, they feel that they have found their other half, the one that completes them and makes them whole.

TANGO

Widower's Tango

Pablo Neruda

1933 & 1935

Oh Maligna, by now you will have found the letter, by now you
will have cried with rage
and you will have insulted the memory of my mother
calling her a rotten bitch and a mother of dogs,
by now you will have drunk alone, all by yourself, your
afternoon tea
with your eyes on my old shoes which are empty forever,
and by now you will not be able to recall my illness, my dreams
at night, my meals
without cursing me out loud as though I were still there
complaining of the tropics, of the coolies corringhis,
of the poisonous fevers which did me such harm,
and of the horrendous English whom I still hate.

Maligna, the truth of it, how vast the night is, how lonely the
earth!
I have gone back again to single bedrooms,
to cold lunches in restaurants, and I
drop my pants and my shirts on the floor as I used to,
there are no hangers in my room, and nobody's pictures are on
the walls.
How much of the shadow that is in my soul I would give to have
you back,
the names of the months sound to me like threats
and the word winter is like the sound of lugubrious drum.

Later on you will find buried near the coconut tree
the knife which I hid there for fear you would kill me,
and now suddenly I would be glad to smell its kitchen steel
used to the weight of your hand, the shine of your foot:
under the dampness of the ground, among the deaf roots.
In all the languages of men only the poor will know your name,
and the dense earth does not understand your name
made of impenetrable divine substances.

Thus it hurts me to think of the clear day of your legs
in repose like waters of the sun made to stay in place,
and the swallow that lives in your eyes sleeping and flying,
and the mad dog that you harbour in your heart,
and thus also I see the dead who are between us and will be
from now on,
and I breathe ash and utter ruin in the air itself,
I would give this giant sea-wind for your sudden breath
and the vast solitary space that will be around me forever.

I would give this wind off the giant sea for your hoarse
breathing
heard in the long nights unmixed with oblivion,
becoming part of the atmosphere as the whip becomes part of
the horse's skin.
And to hear you make water, in the darkness, at the bottom of
the house,
as though you were pouring a slow, tremulous, silvery,
obstinate honey,
how many times over would I yield up this choir of shadows
which I possess,
and the clash of useless swords which is audible in my soul,
and the dove of blood, alone on my forehead,
calling to things which have vanished, to beings who have
vanished,
to substances incomprehensibly inseparable and lost.

UNDRESS

Delta of Venus

Anaïs Nin

1977

"Go to sleep," he said.

She was calmed by his words, in which she detected a shade of pity. But she could not sleep. Her body was keyed up. She knew how the breath changed in sleep, and the movements of the breasts. So she pretended to fall asleep. All the time she felt the hand on her shoulder, and its warmth penetrated right through her clothes. He began to caress her shoulder. He did this so quietly that she was afraid she would fall asleep, but she did not want to lose the pleasant sensation that was running down her spine at the round touch of his hand. She relaxed completely.

He touched her throat and waited. He wanted to be sure that she was asleep. He touched her breasts. Bijou did not stir.

Cautiously, deftly, he caressed her belly, and with a pressure of the finger pushed the black silk of her dress so as to outline the shape of her legs and the space between the legs. When he made this valley clear, he continued to caress the legs. He had not yet touched her legs beyond the dress. Then he noiselessly left his chair, went to the foot of the couch and kneeled down. In this position, Bijou knew, he could look up her dress and see that she wore nothing underneath. He looked for a long while.

Then she felt him lifting the hem of the skirt slightly to be able to see more. Bijou had stretched herself out with her legs slightly parted. She was melting under his touch and his eyes. How wonderful it was to be looked at while apparently asleep, to feel that the man was entirely free. She felt the silk being lifted, felt her legs exposed to the air. He was staring at them.

With one hand he caressed them softly, slowly, enjoying them to the full, feeling the smooth lines, the long silk passage leading up under the dress. Bijou found it difficult to lie absolutely still. She wanted to part her legs a little more. How slowly his hand traveled. She could feel how he followed the contours of the legs, lingering over the curves, how his hand stopped at the knee, then continued. He stopped just before touching the sex. He must have been watching her face to see if she was deeply hypnotized. With two fingers he began to feel her sex, knead it.

When he felt the honey that had been quietly flowing, he slipped his head under the skirt, hid himself between her legs and began to kiss her. His tongue was long and agile, penetrating. She had to restrain herself from moving towards his voracious mouth.

The little lamp gave so dim a light that she risked opening her eyes halfway. He had withdrawn his head from her skirt and was slowly taking off his clothes. He stood near her, magnificent, tall, like some African king, his eyes glowing, his teeth bared, his mouth wet.

VALENTINE

Lunchbox Love Note

Kenn Nesbitt

2010

Inside my lunch
to my surprise
a perfect heart-shaped
love note lies.

The outside says,
"Will you be mine?"
and, "Will you be
my valentine?"

I take it out
and wonder who
would want to tell me
"I love you."

Perhaps a girl
who's much too shy
to hand it to me
eye to eye.

Or maybe it
was sweetly penned
in private by
a secret friend

Who found my lunchbox
sitting by
and slid the note in
on the sly.

Oh, I'd be thrilled
if it were Jo,
the cute one in
the second row.

Or could it be
from Jennifer?
Has she found out
I'm sweet on her?

My mind's abuzz,
my shoulders tense.
I need no more
of this suspense.

My stomach lurching
in my throat,
I open up
my little note.

Then wham! as if
it were a bomb,
inside it reads,
"I love you—Mom."

WISH

Sense and Sensibility

Jane Austen

1811

Not all that Mrs. Bennet, however, with the assistance of her five daughters, could ask on the subject, was sufficient to draw from her husband any satisfactory description of Mr. Bingley. They attacked him in various ways, with barefaced questions, ingenious suppositions, and distant surmises; but he eluded the skill of them all; and they were at last obliged to accept the second-hand intelligence of their neighbour, Lady Lucas. Her report was highly favourable. Sir William had been delighted with him. He was quite young, wonderfully handsome, extremely agreeable, and, to crown the whole, he meant to be at the next assembly with a large party. Nothing could be more delightful! To be fond of dancing was a certain step towards falling in love; and very lively hopes of Mr. Bingley's heart were entertained.

"If I can but see one of my daughters happily settled at Netherfield," said Mrs. Bennet to her husband, "and all the others equally well married, I shall have nothing to wish for."

The Children Act

Ian McEwan

2014

'What do you want, Jack?'

'I'm going to have this affair.'

'You want a divorce.'

'No. I want everything the same. No deception.'

'I don't understand.'

'Yes you do. Didn't you once tell me that couples in long marriages aspire to the condition of siblings? We've arrived, Fiona. I've become your brother. It's cosy and sweet and I love you, but before I drop dead, I want one big passionate affair.'

Mistaking her amazed gasp for laughter, for mockery perhaps, he said roughly, 'Ecstasy, almost blacking out with the thrill of it. Remember that? I want one last go, even if you don't. Or perhaps you do.'

She stared at him in disbelief.

'There it is then.'

This was when she had found her voice and told him what kind of idiot he was. She had a powerful grip on what was conventionally correct. That he had, as far as she knew, always been faithful, made his proposition all the more outrageous. Or if he'd deceived her in the past then he'd done it brilliantly. She already knew the name of the woman. Melanie. Not so remote from the name of a fatal form of skin cancer. She knew she could be obliterated by his affair with this twenty-eight-year-old statistician.

'If you do this it'll be the end for us. It's as simple as that.'

'Is this a threat?'

'My solemn promise.'

X-LOVE

Anna Karenina

Leo Tolstoy

1878

Happy families are all alike; every unhappy family is unhappy in its own way.

Everything was in confusion in the Oblonskys' house. The wife had discovered that the husband was carrying on an intrigue with a French girl, who had been a governess in their family, and she had announced to her husband that she could not go on living in the same house with him. This position of affairs had now lasted three days, and not only the husband and wife themselves, but all the members of their family and household, were painfully conscious of it. Every person in the house felt that there was no sense in their living together, and that the stray people brought together by chance in any inn had more in common with one another than they, the members of the family and household of the Oblonskys. The wife did not leave her own room, the husband had not been at home for three days. The children ran wild all over the house; the English governess quarreled with the housekeeper, and wrote to a friend asking her to look out for a new situation for her; the man-cook had walked off the day before just at dinner time; the kitchen-maid, and the coachman had given warning.

The House of Sleep

Jonathan Coe

1997

It was their final quarrel, that much was clear. But although he had been anticipating it for days, perhaps even for weeks, nothing could quell the tide of anger and resentment which now rose up inside him. She had been in the wrong, and had refused to admit it. Every argument he had attempted to put forward, every attempt to be conciliatory and sensible, had been distorted, twisted around and turned back against him. How dare she bring up that perfectly innocent evening he had spent in The Half Moon with Jennifer? How dare she call his gift 'pathetic', and claim that he was looking 'shifty' when he gave it to her? And how dare she bring up his mother – his mother, of all people – and accuse him of seeing her too often? As if that were some sort of comment on his maturity; on his masculinity, even ...

He stared blindly ahead, unconscious of his surroundings or of his fellow pedestrians. 'Bitch,' he thought to himself, as her words came back to him. And then out loud, through clenched teeth, he shouted, 'BITCH!'

YES

These I Can Promise

author unknown

s.d.

I cannot promise you a life of sunshine;
I cannot promise riches, wealth, or gold;
I cannot promise you an easy pathway
That leads away from change or growing old.
But I can promise all my heart's devotion;
A smile to chase away your tears of sorrow;
A love that's ever true and ever growing;
A hand to hold in yours through each tomorrow.

Hamletmachine

Heiner Müller

1984

HEART PIECE

ONE: May I put my heart at your feet?
TWO: As long as you don't soil my floor.
ONE: My heart is pure.
TWO: We'll see to that.
ONE: I can't get it out.
TWO: You'd like me to help you?
ONE: If you don't mind.
TWO: It is my pleasure.
I too can't get it out.

CRIES

TWO: I'll take out by surgery
What do I have a penknife for.
We'll have this in a minute.
To work and not to despair.
TWO: Well, it's done.
But this is a brick.
Your heart is a brick.
ONE: Yes.
But it beats only for you.

Siberia

Bart Moeyaert

2003

Give me your coat
of teddy bear fur.
Wrap me in your winter clothes
and in your arms.
Kiss me warm.
Kiss me
until I purr.
Then take off your skin
and tuck me in.
Hush me with your heartbeat –
us our, us our, us our –
and turn this outsized double bed
into a tiny keep of eiderdown.

p.6 From *The Unbearable Lightness of Being* by Milan Kundera, first published in 1984 by Gallimard. Reproduced by permission of HarperCollins US / Wylie Agency UK, copyright © Editions Gallimard, 1984 / estate of Milan Kundera, 1984.

p.7 From *Eleanor Oliphant Is Completely Fine: Reese's Book Club: a Novel* by Gail Honeyman, copyright © 2017 by Gail Honeyman. Used by permission of Pamela Dorman Books, an imprint of Penguin Publishing Group, a division of Penguin Random House LLC. and HarperCollins UK. All rights reserved.

p.10 From *Narcissus and Goldmund* by Hermann Hesse, translated by Ursule Molinaro. Copyright © 1930, 1957 by Hermann Hesse, Montagnola, © 1930, Suhrkamp Verlag GmbH, Berlin. Translation © 1968 by Farrar, Straus and Giroux. English translation used by permission of Pushkin Press and Farrar, Straus and Giroux. All rights reserved.

p.11 From *Varieties of Disturbance* by Lydia Davis, copyright © 2007 by Lydia Davis. Used by permission of Farrar, Straus and Giroux and Hamish Hamilton, a division of Penguin Random House LLC. All rights reserved.

p.15 Used by permission of Jan Lauwereyns.

pp.18-19 From *The Hour of the Star* of Clarice Lispector, copyright © 1977 by Clarice Lispector. translated by Benjamin Moser. Used by permission of Agencia Carmen Balcells and Penguin Publishing Group UK, a division of Penguin Random House LLC. All rights reserved.

p.24 From *Levels of Life* by Julian Barnes published by Jonathan Cape, copyright © Julian Barnes, 2013. Reprinted by permission of The Random House Group Limited, of Alfred A. Knopf, an imprint of the Knopf Doubleday Publishing Group, a division of Penguin Random House LLC and of Vintage Canada/Random House Canada, a division of Penguin Random House Canada Limited. All rights reserved.

p.25 *Funeral Blues*, copyright © 1940 by The Estate of W.H. Auden and © renewed 1968 by W. H. Auden; *from Collected Poems* by W. H. Auden, edited by Edward Mendelson. Used by permission of Random House, an imprint and division of Penguin Random House LLC., and of Curtis Brown, Ltd. All rights reserved.

pp.28-29 From *Americanah* by Chimamanda Ngozi Adichie, copyright © 2013 by Chimamanda Ngozi Adichie. Reprinted by permission of HarperCollins UK, of Alfred A. Knopf, an imprint of the Knopf Doubleday Publishing Group, a division of Penguin Random House LLC., and of Vintage Canada/Alfred A. Knopf Canada, a division of Penguin Random House Canada Limited. All rights reserved.

p.32 From *Giovanni's Room* by James Baldwin. Copyright © 1956, renewed 1984 by James Baldwin. Used by permission of Ayesha Pande Literary and the James Baldwin Estate.

p.33 From *Lie With Me* by Philippe Besson published by Penguin. Copyright © Editions Julliard, Paris, 2017 English Translation Copyright © Ringwald Inc, 2019. Reprinted by permission of Penguin Books Limited and of Simon & Schuster US.

pp.36-37 From Valeria Luiselli, *Allegoric lot no 3*, translated by Christina MacSweeney, from *The Story of My Teeth: A Novel*, copyright © 2015 by Valeria Luiselli. Translation copyright © 2015 by Christina MacSweeney. Reprinted with the permission of The Permissions Company, LLC on behalf of Coffee House Press, coffeehousepress.org and Granta Books.

p.40 From *The Infatuations* by Javier Marías, copyright © Javier Marías, 2012, translation copyright © Margaret Jull Costa, 2012. Reprinted by permission of Hamish Hamilton, an imprint of Penguin Publishing Group, and Casanovas & Lynch. All rights reserved.

p.44 From *The Story of a New Name* by Elena Ferrante, copyright © Elena Ferrante, 2012, translation copyright © Ann Goldstein. Reprinted by permission of Europa Editions Ltd. All rights reserved.

p.45 From *The Dangers of Smoking in Bed: Stories* by Mariana Enriquez, translated by Megan McDowell, translation copyright © 2021 by Penguin Random House LLC. Used by permission of Hogarth, an imprint of Random House, a division of Penguin Random House LLC, and of Granta Books. All rights reserved.

p.48 From *Conversations with Friends* by Sally Rooney, copyright © Sally Rooney, 2017. Used by permission of Sally Rooney, Faber and Faber

Ltd and Crown Publishing Group, a division of Penguin Random House LLC. All rights reserved.

p.57 From *Open Water*, published by Viking. Copyright © 2021 by Caleb Azumah Nelson. Used by permission of Grove/Atlantic, Inc and of Penguin Books Limited. Any third-party use of this material, outside of this publication, is prohibited. All rights reserved.

p.60 From *American Psycho* by Brett Easton Ellis, first published in 1991 by Picador, a division of Macmillan Publishers International Limited. Reproduced by permission of Macmillan Publishers International Limited, London, and of Vintage Books, an imprint of the Knopf Doubleday Publishing Group, a division of Penguin Random House LLC. All rights reserved. Copyright © Brett Easton Ellis 1991.

p.61 From *Mythos* by Stephen Fry © Stephen Fry, 2017, published by Penguin, reproduced by kind permission of David Higham Associates.

p.64 From *Girl, Woman Other* published by Hamish Hamilton, copyright © 2019 by Bernadine Evaristo. Used by permission of Grove/Atlantic, Inc and of Penguin Books Ltd. Any third-party use of this material, outside of this publication, is prohibited. All rights reserved.

p.68 From *Another roadside attraction* by Tom Robbins, copyright © 1990 by Tom Robbins. Used by permission of Bantam Books, an imprint of Random House, a division of Penguin Random House LLC. All rights reserved.

p.69 English Translation, by Justin O'Brien, copyright © 1955, copyright renewed 1983 by Penguin Random House LLC; and Excerpt(s) from *The myth of Sisyphus* by Albert Camus, translated by Justin O'Brien, copyright 1942 by Librairie Gallimard. English translation copyright © 1955, copyright renewed 1983 by Penguin Random House LLC. Used by permission of Alfred A. Knopf, an imprint of the Knopf Doubleday Publishing Group, a division of Penguin Random House LLC and of Penguin Classics, a division of Penguin Books UK. All rights reserved.

p.73 © Peter Verhelst, 2008, originally published in *Nieuwe sterrenbeelden*, published by Prometheus, Amsterdam, copyright translation © Poetry International.

p.80 From *Embers* by Sándor Márai, translation 2001 by Carol Brown Janeway. Used by permission of Alfred A. Knopf, an imprint of the Knopf Doubleday Publishing Group, a division of Penguin Random House LLC. All rights reserved.

pp.84-85 Pablo Neruda, "Tango del viudo", *Residencia en la tierra*, © Pablo Neruda 1933 & 1935 and Fundación Pablo Neruda. Translated by Lewis Hyde, 2001, The Kenyon Review, Vol. 23, Issue 2.

pp.88-89 From *Delta of Venus* by Anaïs Nin. Used by permission of Penguin Classics, a division of Penguin Random House LLC and HarperCollins US. All rights reserved.

pp.92-93 From *When The Teacher Isn't Looking* by Kenn Nesbitt, copyright © 2010. Reprinted by permission of Running Press Adult, an imprint of Hachette Book Group, Inc.

p.97 From *The Children Act* by Ian McEwan published by Jonathan Cape. Copyright © Ian McEwan, 2014. Reprinted by permission of The Random House Group Limited, of Alfred A. Knopf Canada, a division of Penguin Random House Canada Limited, and of Nan A. Talese, an imprint of the Knopf Doubleday Publishing Group, a division of Penguin Random House LLC.. All rights reserved.

p.101 From *The House of Sleep* by Jonathan Coe, copyright © 1997 by Jonathan Coe. Used by permission of Viking Books UK, a division of The Random House Group Limited, Alfred A. Knopf, an imprint of the Knopf Doubleday Publishing Group, a division of Penguin Random House LLC, and of Felicity Bryan Associates. All rights reserved.

p.105 ©1984 copyright by Performing Arts Journal Publications, ©1984 copyright Carl Weber for Translation, Introduction, and Interview with Heiner Müller, ©copyright of plays in the original held by Suhrkamp Verlag, Berlin, Germany.

p.108 Originally published in *Verzamel de liefde* by Bart Moeyaert, published by Querido, 2006, translated by David Colmer.

All mentioned dates in this book are first publication dates of the original work.

Sanny Winters (born 1975) and her partner form
the graphic design duo Oeyen & Winters.
As a visual artist, she has previously published the books *A City*, *Belgium Xtra Bold*, *Gent Xtra Bold* and *Mirror*.
Her love of letters and of love itself come together in this new book.

♥

For a selection of the most beautiful excerpts from world literature,
Sanny called on her close friend Silvie Moors.
Silvie Moors (born 1975) studied Germanic language and literature.
She loves reading and people, and places where the two come together.
She is a reading promoter, literary moderator and 'book doctor'.

Book design / Tim Oeyen and Sanny Winters

D/2025/45/558 - THEMA: AFF, AKL, AKD
ISBN: 978-90-599-6039-8